TiVo settles patent lawsuit with Verizon for at least $250 million, is ...
www.engadget.com/.../tivo-settles-patent-lawsuit-with-veriz...
by Richard Lawler - in 1,419 Google+ circles - More by Richard Lawler
Sep 24, 2012 – While some patent lawsuits continue to drag on, the battle
between TiVo and Verizon over DVR technology has come to a resolution.

Verizon To Pay TiVo $250M To Settle Patent Lawsuit | Cable ...
www.multichannel.com/news.../verizon-pay...patent-lawsuit/139417
Sep 24, 2012 – Verizon Communications will pay TiVo at least $250 million to settle the
DVR company's pending patent litigation, and the companies are also ...

This search (below) will find news or discussions where Dell has partnered with other companies.

    allintitle: "Dell and * partner"

Dell and Microsoft partner to deliver "open" turn-key cloud solutions ...
commweb-ps3.us.dell.com › Blogs › Enterprise › Inside Enterprise IT
Nov 6, 2010 – Dell and Microsoft partner to deliver "open" turn-key cloud solutions.
Dell.com » Community » Blogs » Enterprise » Inside Enterprise IT » Dell ...

Desktop Virtualization Just Got Simpler – Dell and Citrix Partner for ...
blogs.citrix.com/.../desktop-virtualization-just-got-simpler-dell-and-ci...
Mar 10, 2011 – Desktop Virtualization Just Got Simpler – Dell and Citrix Partner for an
End-to-End Desktop Virtualization Solution. By Natalie Lambert ...

My next stop is LinkedIn where I will do a company search. In this case, I look up the LinkedIn Company page for Microsoft. I do this by adding "Microsoft" in the search box and choosing "Companies" as my search option. (See red arrow?) Once there, I click on the "Insights" link. (See blue arrow.) In the right hand sidebar is a section called "Where Employees Came From." (See black arrow.)

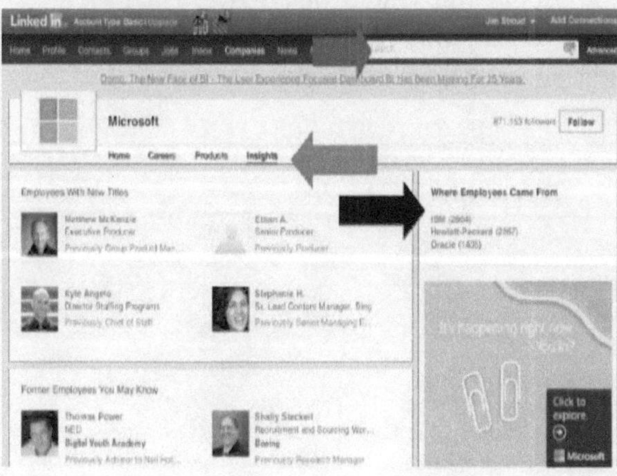

Based on the data on LinkedIn profiles of Microsoft employees, they tend to come from IBM, Hewlett Packard and Oracle. Incidentally, on this LinkedIn company page I can also see what are the most popular skills of Microsoft employees and which Microsoft employees are the most recommended. Good info to know.

Hmm… There is a lot of good info I can use here. When I search on a keyword, I get a list of related skills (**a**), companies that are related to that term in some way (**b**), data on how often that term has been searched on inside LinkedIn (**c**), a list of people who feature this keyword on their profiles (**d**) and a definition of the keyword (**e**). If you were to scroll down this same page, there would be even more great data.

PRESEARCH: DO THE RESEARCH BEFORE YOU SOURCE

SCENARIO: Hiring Manager wants you to find some talent for a specific requisition. Ideally, your meeting with them to discuss their request will happen after you have done the following.

INTERVIEW A CO-WORKER IN THE ROLE

What do they do everyday?

What helps them to be successful on their job? (Skills? Knowledge?)

What are tools they use everyday?

The people who work alongside them, what do they do?

What are typical problems they deal with on the job?

What did they do before working at your company?

What personality traits would be helpful to excel on their job?

ANALYZE RESUMES IN YOUR ATS

Interview a co-worker in the role

Who was interviewed previously for the role?

Where did they come from?

Why were they turned down?

If they were merely outshined, will the manager reconsider them?

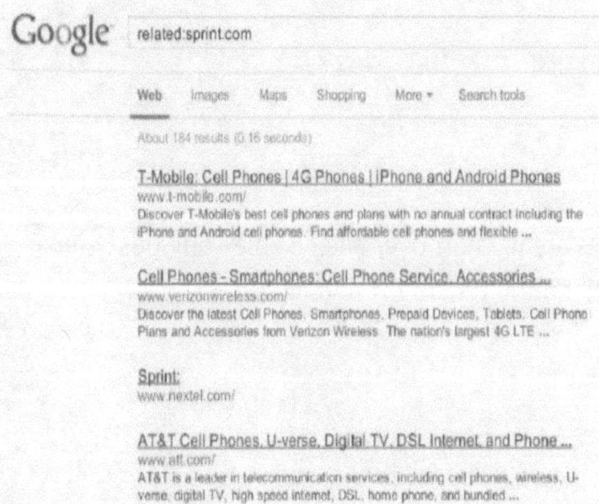

I'll get more into this later when I focus on Google specific search

commands. For now, suffice to say, I am asking Google to find companies that are related to Sprint. As such, these would be competitor companies and/or companies operating in their space. For example: T-Mobile, Verizon, ATT and MetroPCS.

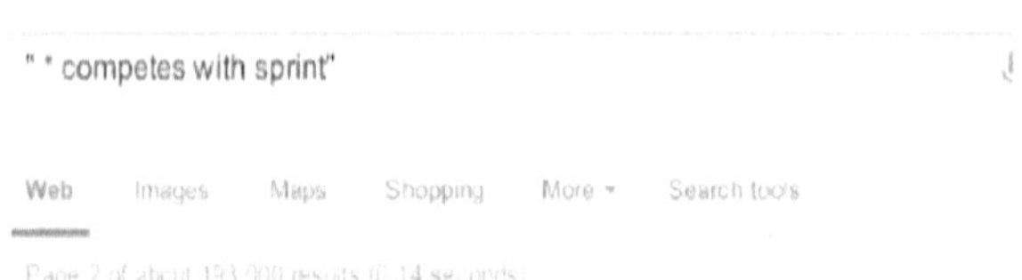

In the search string above, I am asking Google to fill in the blank for my search. This is the function of the asterix in Google searches. As a result, Google is finding search results that fit the pattern of what I am looking for. As you can see in the search results below, the following companies compete with Sprint: Clearwire, VoiceStream and Leap.

Hmm… If companies are in court over patents, they obviously have similar tech. This is what my search (below) is looking for.

verizon patent litigation

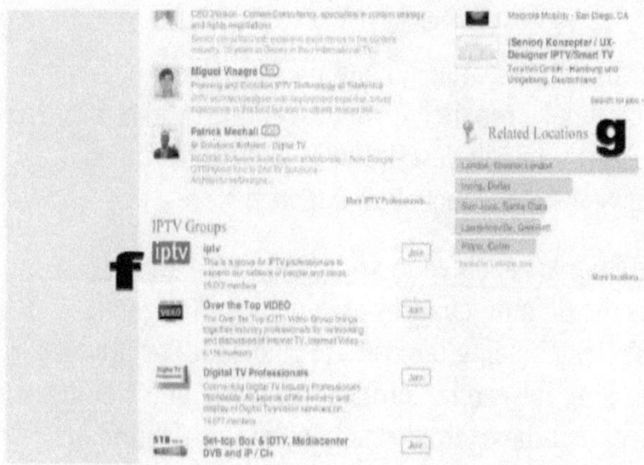

LinkedIn is kind enough to give me a list of LinkedIn Groups dedicated to the keyword I am researching (**f**) and a list of locations (**g**). How does that work? To my knowledge, people who have the keyword I am searching for (in this case, IPTV) on their profile, tend to live in London, Dallas, Lawrenceville (GA), San Jose (CA) and so on.

After all of the previous research has been done, I take a good look at the job description. (Go figure.)

What are the keywords and phrases from the job description that will likely be on a candidate's resume?

How does your competition title similar jobs? For example, is a Digital Strategist at your company the same thing as a Social Media Strategist

somewhere else?

\# Take out a thesaurus and research synonyms. "Troubleshoot" may be in the job description but, "make repairs" is on the resume. Make sense?

\# What tools are listed in the job description? Make a list of competing tools. How? I have a suggestion. (Pun intended.)

If you have Google Suggest enabled in your Google Search preferences (and since it is the default, chances are you do), Google autocompletes your searches. Such being the case, to find a tool or product that competes with another, simply search: "product name vs" and Google will list rival products. Check out the examples below for clarification on what I mean.

java vs **javascript**

java vs **c++**

java vs **python**

java vs **.net**

---

asp vs **php**

asp vs **asp.net**

asp vs **saas**

asp vs **.net**

python vs

python vs **ruby**

python vs **php**

python vs **perl**

python vs **java**

After doing all of the previous research, you should be more than prepared when meeting with the hiring manager about the role. Below are a few examples of how I imagine your chat may progress.

A) My research tells me that candidates we have interviewed in the past come from Company A and Company B. Companies X and Y are similar to Companies A & B. Such being the case, are you open to candidates from Companies X and Y and others similar to them?

B) I have noticed that Company G and Company V has tech that is similar to ours. Do you want to see candidates from these companies?

C) My research tells me that these types of candidates tend to live in Atlanta, Chicago and New York. Is relocation an option for the right candidate?

D) Would you consider candidates with alternative skills? For example, software Q competes with software X in the marketplace. If I present candidates skilled in software X instead of Q, would you be open to speaking with them?

E) If I presented you with a list of related skills that I think may help me in finding candidates for you, would you review it to see if I am on target?

F) I have noticed that our competitor has a job called (insert job title here) that is very similar in scope to our job (insert job title here). Such being the case, shall I assume that you are open to viewing (competitor job title) resumes as well?

G) Whenever possible, I will give preference to those candidates that meet certain personality criteria. My research tells me that people who are quick learners and have an eye for detail will excel in this role. Is this your assertion as well?

H) My research tells me that before someone takes on this job title, they are either job title one, job title two or job title three. If I found someone with enough relevant experience in those roles, would you consider them?

I) I think you have it from here.

;-)

OMG! THIS IS A LOT OF WORK!

If this seems like a lot of work that's because it is a lot of work; however, it is SO worth it. It will save you time by helping you present quality candidates verses a deluge of resumes. Make sense? Plus, Hiring Managers will appreciate you more.

QUICK TIP

Keep research on all the jobs you source for. This will make it easier for other recruiters sourcing for similar jobs.

SOURCING INSIDE THE MAJORS

In this section, I will focus on search methods that will work on Google, Yahoo and Bing. I will also touch on being efficient.

I love me some Google. However, it is necessary to search multiple search engines because there is less than 1% overlap in search engine results.

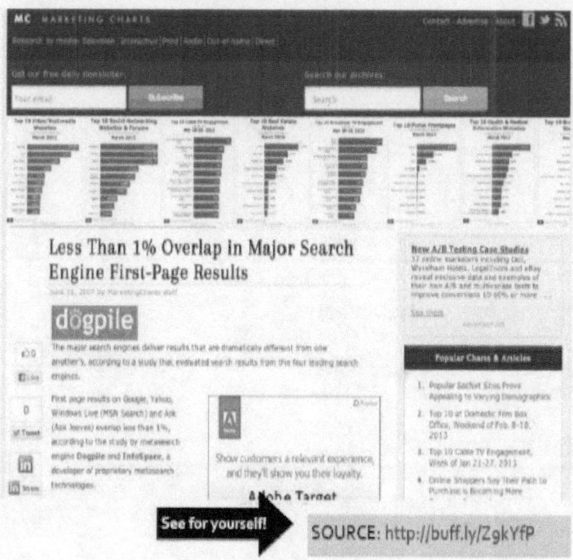

UNIVERSAL SYNTAX

All search engines are not the same. However in some instances, there is a shared language. These commands work on Google, Yahoo and Bing.

inurl: searches for a keyword in the URL of a web document.
intitle: Searches for a keyword in the title of a web document.
site: Restricts search results to a particular domain.
filetype: Restricts results to a particular format. (i.e. PDF, DOCX)
- The minus sign restricts a keyword of phrase from your results.
" " Quotes asks the search engine to find an exact phrase.

In this example, I am asking Google to search the Lockheed Martin website for mentions of the phrase "Principal Engineer." Among the results: Robert Szczerba, Gary Wroblewski and Steve Moraites. If I were recruiting Principal Engineers, I might reach out to them. Just sayin'…

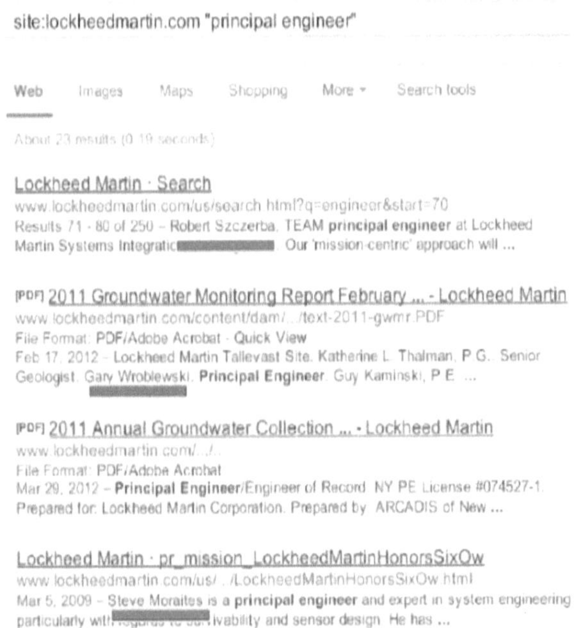

In the example below, I am looking for a radar engineer with DOD experience. I do not want the words "submit," "apply," "your," "sample," or "example" in my results as they typically would be on the job descriptions.

By the way, I added a period between the words "resume" and "of." I very well could have searched the same results if I searched this way:

intitle:resume.of radar engineer ("department of defense"
OR DOD) -submit -apply -your -sample -example

Just fyi…

In the screenshot below, I am looking for an engineer with a background in missiles. I could go on ad nauseum with these search examples. (Ooh, aren't I fancy?)

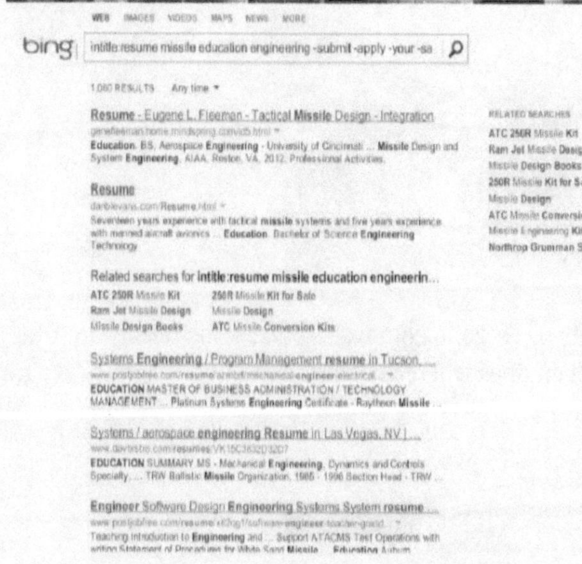

The search is cut off in the picture. This is the full search string.

intitle:resume missile education engineering -submit -apply
-your -sample -example

Now, let me show you something really cool that pushes my point about using more than one search engine even further.

A metasearch engine is a search engine that searches search engines and Dogpile.com is one. Specifically, it searches Google, Yahoo and Yandex. In the example below I am searching for the phrase "natural language processing" on resumes that are cited on college websites.

In the search results of Dogpile.com we see that some results are exclusive to certain search engines whereas others are shared.

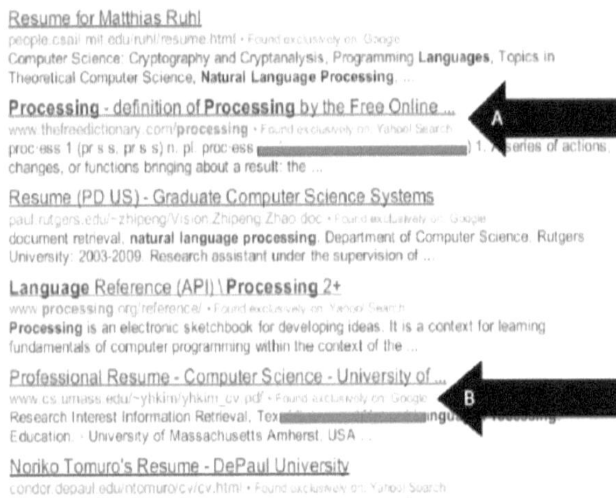

Search result A is exclusive to Yahoo. Search result B is exclusive to Google. Just in case you missed it, I have underlined the language in red where it says, "Found exclusively on..."

Although I did not scan beyond the first couple of pages of results, chances are that I would find search results that are exclusive to Yandex as well. And for those who don't know, Yandex is a search engine based in Russia. Its very popular in certain circles. Hah! I can just imagine the look on some of your faces.

Oh yeah! There are definitely more search engines than the big three: Google, Yahoo and Bing. Hmm… Maybe that's a subject for another book? Yeah, that sounds right. For now, let me share with you search commands that are exclusive to Google.

* WILDCARD

Google refers to the asterix as the "wildcard." The wildcard commands asks Google to fill in the blank. In the example above, notice how Google finds search results that fits where a missing word is. In one case, "test" and in another, "Development." (As shown below.)

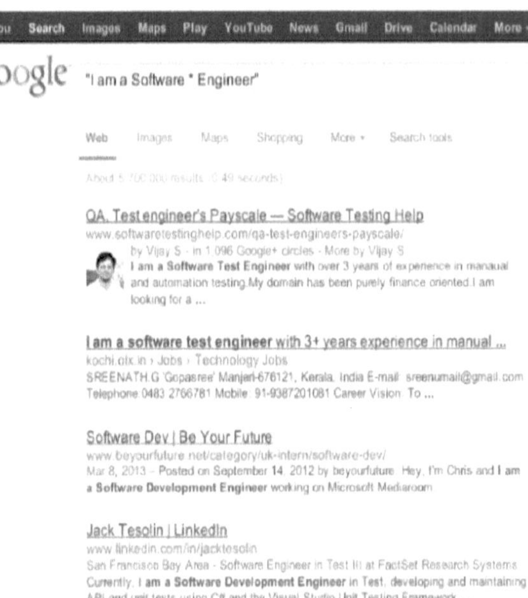

~ TILDE

This is the tilde. When you add it in front of a keyword on Google, it looks for synonyms and/or similar words. In the example above, notice how certain words are bolded? Google thinks the words: career, employment, job and resume are related to the word "job."

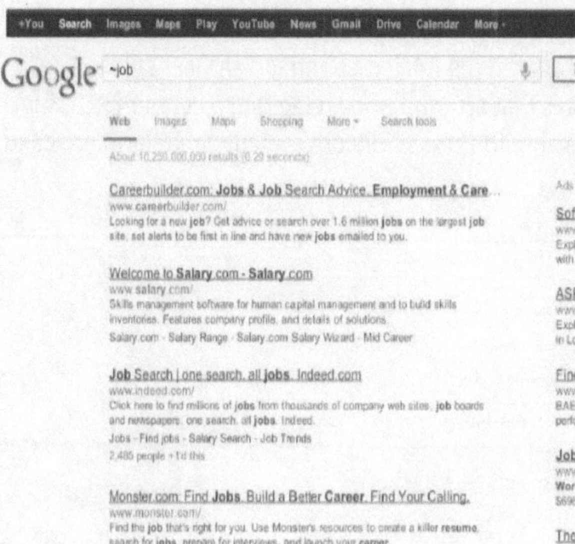

.. NUMRAGE

The numrange commands is represented in the two dots. It allows you to search within a range of numbers. In the example above, I am looking for resumes that have 2006-present, 2007-present, 2008-present, 2009-present, 2010-present or 2011-present cited therein.

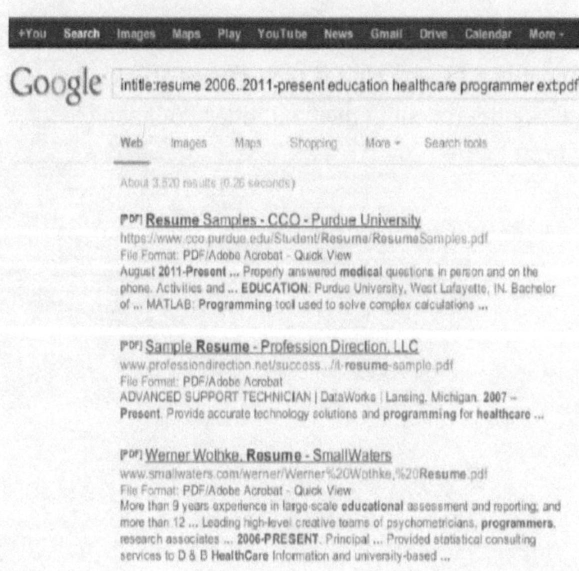

RELATED

If you remember, I shared the related command earlier. This command looks for websites that are similar or related to a certain URL. In this case, websites that are akin to Prudential.com include StateFarm.com and AllState.com.

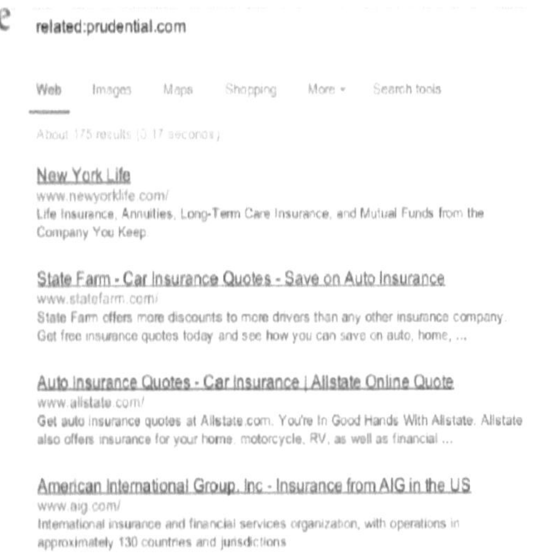

ALLINTITLE

The allintitle command says that all the keywords must appear in the title of the page. The EXT command I am using is the same as "filetype." Notice how the search terms are not touching the "allintitle" command? (Unlike how EXT is being used.)

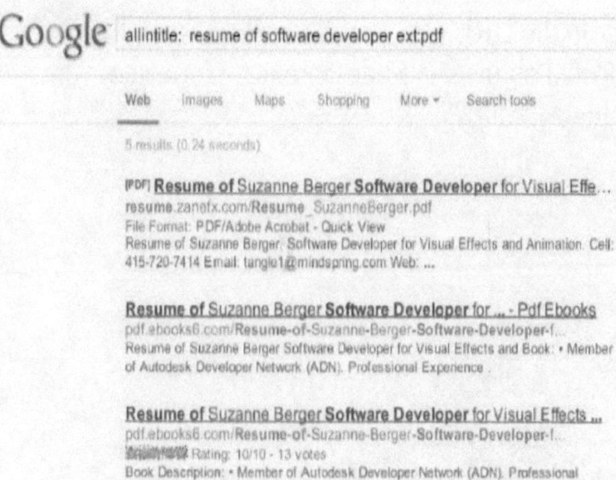

ALLINTEXT

With the "allintext" command, you are asking Google to insure that all of the query words must appear in the text of the page. (Part of the search in the screenshot is hidden. The missing part is "references upon request."). Notice how the search terms are not touching "allintext?"

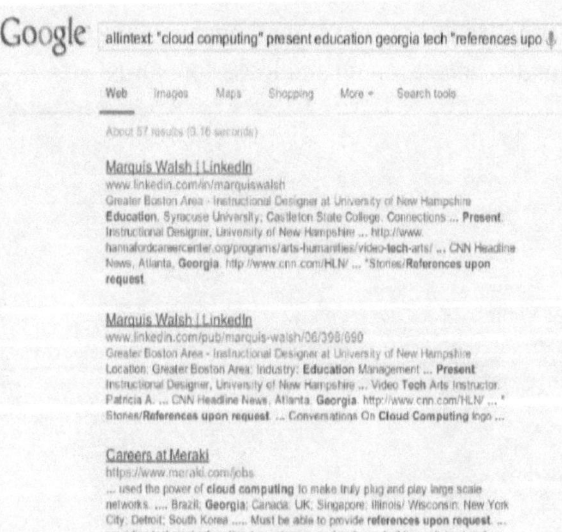

ALLINURL

The "allinurl" commands says all query words (in this case "resume of slideshare") must appear in the URL of a search result. Above, I am seeking resumes that are posted on the site Slideshare.net. Notice how the search terms are not touching "allinurl?"

Google   allinurl: resume of slideshare

INTEXT

The "intext" command says that the terms must appear in the text of the page. (Searching without the "intext" command looks for words anywhere on the page.)

Google   intext:hotmail.com intext:programming intext:expected.graduation.date extc

LINK

The "link" command (below) is being used to find pages that link to https://developers.google.com. TIP: Finding sites that interest developers is a way of finding developers. Just sayin'.

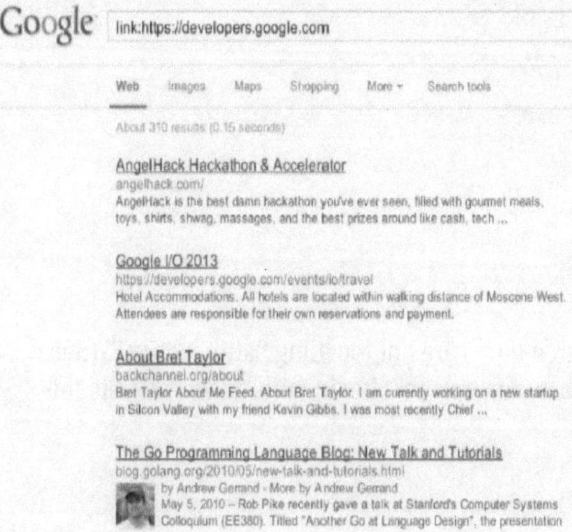

ALLINANCHOR

REMINDER: Finding sites that interest developers is a way of finding developers. In the above, I am using the "allinanchor" command to find links that have all of the words "useful java code" in them.

Notice how the search terms are not touching "allinanchor?" (See above.) Pretty much search commands that begin with "allin" operate this way.

INANCHOR

The "inanchor" command says that he terms must appear in the text of links on the page. (Above, notice the search words in the title.)

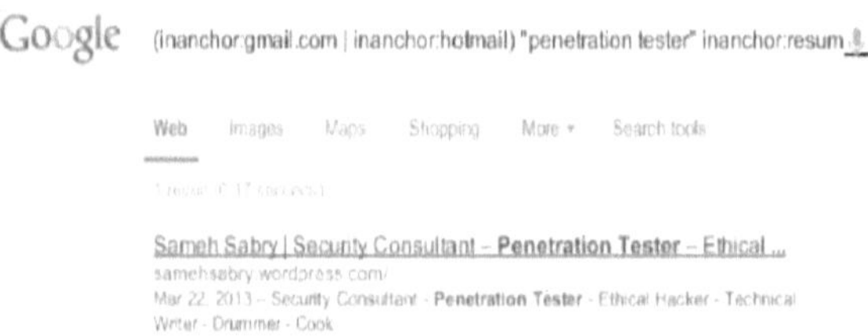

* Quick side note: (keyword | keyword) is the same as searching (keyword OR keyword). The symbol I am using for "OR" in the screenshot is called the pipe command. Don't want to confuse you.   ;-)

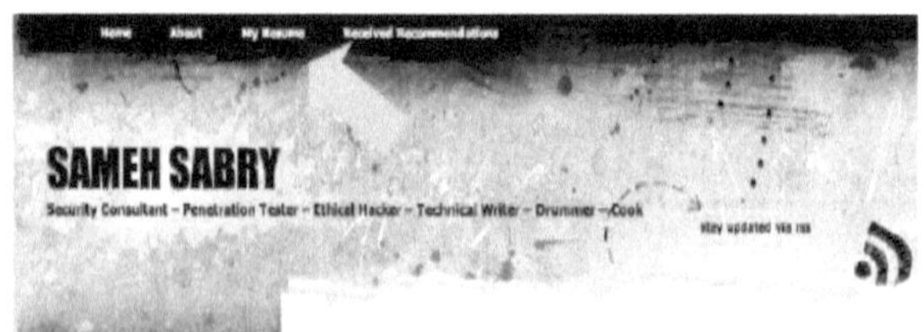

In the top image I am looking for a "penetration tester" on a page that has the keywords gmail or hotmail in a link. Also, the word "resume" is in a link as well. After the search, there was only one result. On that resulting page, there is a "my resume" link at the top (see arrow) and a link to a blog post about Hotmail (not shown above). Good, but I was hoping for an email address. Oh well.

…

WHOA! Starting to feel information overload? Well, that's the advantage of having this is in a book. You can always put it down and come back to it.

…

Well, just in case you do not have information overload (and even if you do), here is a list of keywords and phrases you can use to find free resumes on Google. They are basically, a list of words typical to resumes and job descriptions. Enjoy!

EXCLUDE THE FOLLOWING JOB DESCRIPTION KEYWORDS IN YOUR SEARCHES

Apply	careers	Benefits	recruiter
Request	reply	wizard	recruit
Templates	preferred	free	download
Template	example	your	tips
Jobs	submit	paste	hiring
Job	eoe	search	"looking for"
Post	"equal opportunity employer"	order	
Sample	send	openings	

INCLUDE THE FOLLOWING KEYWORDS IN YOUR RESUME SEARCHES

Education	summary	objective	references	experience
Hobbies	personal	references	GPA	volunteer
Phone	email	certifications	internship	cv
Vitae	responsibilities	Awards/honors	academic	overview

INCLUDE THESE COMMON PHRASES IN YOUR RESUME SEARCHES

"managing a staff"   "to gain employment"   "proven track record"
"my years"   "available upon request"   "Team player"
"extensive experience"   "expected graduation date"   "Problem Solver"
"a position that will allow me" "in applying for this position" "fast paced"
"I will be utilizing"   "results oriented"   Entrepreneurial
Dynamic   Highly motivated   Communication skills
"track record"   "problem solving"| analytical
Effective   specialized   detail oriented

"salary negotiable"   "Responsible for"   "Experience working in"   "self starter"
"hard working"   "performance oriented"   "committed to excellence" "solutions oriented"
"Positive attitude"   "quick learner"   "work ethic"   "go to person"

"Track record of success"   "served as company spokesperson"
"managed cross functional teams"   "strong communication skills"
"leadership skills"   "expert presenter"
"Assisted with"   "worked with"
"helped with"   "top ranked"
"Increased revenue by"   "Exceeded goals by"
"decreased costs by"   "Exceeded quotas by"
"fast paced environment"   "company's bottom line"

INCLUDE CUSTOM KEYWORDS AND PHRASES IN YOUR RESUME SEARCHES

Make a list of keywords and phrases specific to your recruiting needs. To include the following:

Job Titles (that your company uses)
Job Titles (that your competition uses)
Competing Companies
Companies with similar technology
Schools (Your candidates attended)
Area Codes (for location specific requisitions)
Zip Codes (for location specific requisitions)
Associations
Acronyms
Degrees
Certifications
Alternative skill words from the job description
Skill words related to keywords in job description

. . .

NOTE TO SELF: Hmm... How useful is this stuff if they can't apply it to their every day use? I know! I will list a few search scenarios and share how I would resolve them. Yeah, that makes sense.

. . .

RESUME SEARCH STRINGS: JUST ADD KEYWORDS

Below are a list of example search strings and the logic behind them.

To apply them to your needs, simply change the word "keyword" in the search string to whatever keyword is relevant to your need. Also, change the word "job title" in the example below to the job title relevant to your search and so on. Add as many keywords as you like! Experiment, experiment, experiment.

Be careful to add the search into Google EXACTLY as written for the best results. Take note where words are touching a colon. For example, intitle:resume is how your search should be queried and NOT intitle: resume.

Keep in mind also that there are some cases where words are not touching a search command such as, when I use the "allintitle" command. For example: allintitle: planes trains automobiles. That being said, pay very close attention to how I have written these examples. Cool? Cool.

…

I want to look for resumes where the authorship is claimed. For example, Alan Smith's resume. I also do not want to see examples of resumes. Neither do I want documents that have the word "submit" in them because that word is typically on a job description. For example, "if you are interested in this job, click here to submit your resume." Get it? This is how I would find resumes that meet that criteria.

```
intitle:"*'s resume" keyword –intitle:examples
–intitle:sample –intitle:submit
```

I want to find curriculum vitaes. So, I look for terms related to curriculum vitae in the title of a document. I don't want job descriptions in my results, so I restrict the words "apply" and "submit" from being in any link. Why? More often than not, on a job description those words would be linking to a career page. I also don't want the word "jobs" in the title of a web document because that is a popular word in the title of career pages. I have also added the word "education" as that is a word that is on most resumes. (smile)

```
(intitle:curriculum.vitae OR inurl:vitae OR intitle:vitae)
"job title"  keyword  keyword  education  -intitle:jobs
-inanchor:apply  -inanchor:submit
```

I am looking for resumes of college students in Atlanta who have a background in computer science. I do not want search results explaining how to do something in computer science, so I restrict the word "how" from the title of returned documents. For that matter, I do not want information about how to write a resume, so I restrict the word "write" from the title of returned documents. Finally, I restrict my search results to websites that end in "edu" because I want resumes that have been posted on a college server.

```
(intitle:"resume for" OR intitle:"resume of")   atlanta
"computer science"  −inanchor:apply    -inanchor:submit
-inanchor:sample  -intitle:how  -intitle:write    site:edu
```

I am looking for a Sales executive in Houston who is a great producer and who has managed teams.   In the search string below, I am looking for a set of words that would be included on such a resume. Notice that I am using the tilde symbol in front of the word "executive" as I am looking not only for the word executive but words related to that as well. For example, words like: management and/or director.

```
allintext:   (summary OR objective) education "leadership
skills"  "exceeded quota"  sales  ~executive  present
houston
```

Below is another way I would seek out a Sales executive in Houston.

```
allintext:  "increased revenue by"  exceeded   education
(sales OR "business development")  houston  (summary OR
objective  OR skills)
```

This is a third attempt to find a Sales person in Houston. Notice how I have the tilde in front of TX? This tells Google to find documents that cite various areas inside of TX. I have also added multiple area codes to the search as well. Why? Often people will add their phone numbers to their resumes.

intitle:resume sales ("exceeded quota" OR "proven track record" OR "bottom line") education ~TX (281 OR 713 OR 832) email -intitle:sample -intitle:example

People also list their full address on their resumes from time to time as well. In the search below, I am using the numrange command to find results with zip codes that are based in Houston, TX.

77002..77012 intitle:resume sales quota

...

Think you got the gist of it? Well, guess what? Surprise! There is a bit more to it. Let me share some tips on finding resumes your competition is overlooking.

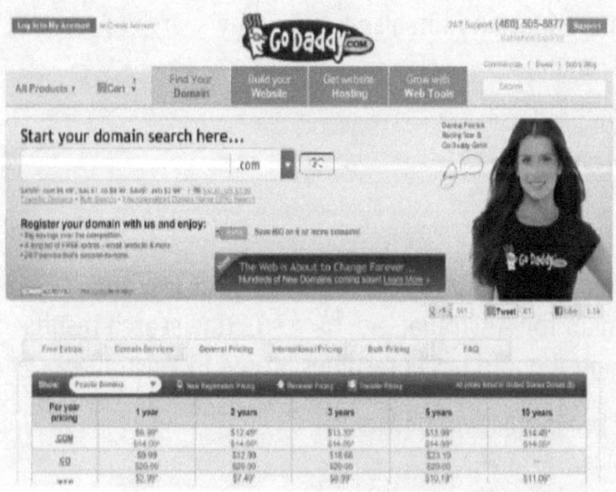

When you don't know a web address, you automatically think (whatever the name is) dot com. Right? I do too. But, there are a lot of top-level domains out there. And said domains, also contain resumes. NOTE: GoDaddy sells hosting and domain registrations. Among the top level domains (TLD) they sell registration on are: .com, .net, .org, .us, .biz, .name and others.

TOP LEVEL DOMAINS

.COM	.NAME	.WS	.PRO	BIZ	.CC	.US.COM
.NET	.INFO	.COM.CO	.US	.ME	.TV	.EDU
.ORG	.CO	.NET.CO				

Above is a list of some top-level domains you may want to experiment with for sourcing resumes. It is by no means an exhaustive list of options. Below are three search string examples to get your creative juices flowing. In the first search string, I am looking for the phrase "my resume" in a link on a web page or in the title. I am also excluding potential job descriptions and resume templates. Finally, I am limiting my search to documents on certain top-level domains.

```
inanchor:my.resume  keyword "job title" city education
present –jobs –apply –submit  -required –wanted
–template  –wizard  –free  –write  –sample  (site:net  OR
site:name OR site:org)
```

In the string below, I am looking for resumes that are formatted in either PDF or word document format. I am also limiting my search to documents on the ".CC" domain.

```
intitle:resume  "job title"  "company  name"     keyword
keyword  (filetype:pdf OR filetype:doc)  -jobs -apply -submit
–required  –wanted  –write  –sample  site:cc
```

By the way, every country has a top-level domain. For example, ".AU" is the top level domain for Australia. So, by restricting search results to documents on that domain, I could target resumes hosted in Australia.

```
site:au  intitle:vitae  keyword keyword keyword  education
-inanchor:submit  -inanchor:apply  ext:pdf
```

NOTE: You can find a list of country-specific top-level domains at: www.iana.org/domains/root/db

...

RESUME SPELLINGS

Did you know that there is more than one way to spell "resume?" Different spellings will result in different search results. Check out the searches I did below and the results.

intitle:resume programmer education –sample –your –apply
-template [840,000 results]

intitle:résumé programmer education –sample –your –apply
-template [13,700 results]

intitle:resumé programmer education –sample –your –apply
-template [2,310 results]

RESUME WRITERS

Resume Writers tend to use common formats when crafting work histories. Their customers tend not to make changes to the documents and upload them to the web as is. Such being the case, a search for certain resume formats will yield results that are often overlooked.

intitle:elegant.resume   education keyword keyword
present (ext:doc | ext:pdf)   -inanchor:submit
-inanchor:apply   -intext:sample   -intext:apply

intitle:functional.resume education keyword keyword
present (ext:doc | ext:pdf) -inanchor:submit
-inanchor:apply -intext:sample -intext:apply

intitle:academic.resume education keyword keyword
keyword present (ext:doc | ext:pdf) -inanchor:submit
-inanchor:apply -intext:sample -intext:apply

intitle:chronological.resume keyword keyword education
present (ext:doc | ext:pdf) -inanchor:submit
-inanchor:apply -intext:sample -intext:apply

ACRONYMS

Some candidates do not list acronyms on their resumes but instead, spell out the abbreviation fully. Case in point, check out the different results between these two searches. Below I am looking for the phrase "extensible markup language" on a resume or vitae but, I do not want the keyword "xml" to appear on the resume. I find only a few resumes this way but, they were most likely overlooked previously by my competition.

```
(intitle:vitae  OR  intitle:resume)  education  -sample
extensible.markup.language -xml -apply -submit  -template
[ 23 results ]
```

When I seek out resumes with the acronym "XML" and restrict documents that contain the phrase it stands for, I get many more. Oh! By the way, I asked Google to restrict documents that had XML in the title as well as I was getting results I did not want. Go figure.

```
(intitle:vitae OR intitle:resume)  education  intext:XML
-extensible.markup.language  -intitle:xml -apply -submit
-sample -template [ 16,200 results ]
```

Let's try a similar search, shall we? Just to bring this point on home. When I look for "Microsoft Office Sharepoint Server" on a resume and restrict reference to its common acronym "MOSS," I only get a few results.

```
(intitle:vitae OR intitle:resume) education  "microsoft
office sharepoint server" -MOSS  -apply -submit  -sample
-template  [ 83 results ]
```

Of course, the inverse brings back what I expected, lots and lots more resumes in comparison. Be advised that I added the keyword "sharepoint" in the search below. Why? I was getting a lot of resumes from people whose name was "Moss." Adding sharepoint to the mix did not wholly cancel that out but, it did give me more of what I wanted to see. Just fyi…

```
(intitle:vitae OR intitle:resume) education MOSS sharepoint
-microsoft.office.sharepoint.server -apply -submit  -sample
-template [ 148,000 results ]
```

NATURAL LANGUAGE

Another way to find passive candidates is not to look for resumes but instead, look for phrases said online. You might be amazed by the number of people you can find searching the web with this technique. Think about it. How many people are online talking about the work they do on their blog or inside of a forum? Below are a few things I found when I searched on "I work at Google."

Dan Russell's Home Page & Site
sites.google.com/site/dmrussell/
I work at Google. I write. I analyze. I experiment. I do field studies and I try to
understand what makes Google users tick. Why do they sometimes query Google for ...

Life at Google – The Microsoftie Perspective | Just Say \"No\" To ...
no2google.wordpress.com/.../life-at-google-the-microsoftie-perspecti...
Jun 24, 2007 – I used to work at Microsoft, now I **work at Google**. Much in this post is
accurate, but mostly it is irrelevant. Engineers join Google and love ...

I work at Google and want to refer software engineers. Anyone ...
www.reddit.com/r/.../i_work_at_google_and_want_to_refer_softwar...
Nov 19, 2012 – I'm looking to refer software engineers for the NY office. I figure I spend
a lot of time on Reddit so maybe there are other people like me on here.

Mike Stay - Google+ - I **work at Google** on the Caja project [1] and I ...
https://plus.google.com/.../posts/VxXav78ZDpm
by Mike Stay - in 810 Google+ circles - More by Mike Stay
Dec 15, 2012 – I **work at Google** on the Caja project [1] and I'm a PhD student
at U. of Auckland. Cris Calude and John Baez (at UC Riverside) are my
advisors; ...

Here are a few more searches for you to try.

CANDIDATES DISCUSSING THEIR WORK

"I am a job title"
"I graduated from school" keyword
"I work in a keyword" lab
"I work at company name"
"I love company name"
"I hate company name"
"I reported to * " "at work"
"We have been working on * for years"

COMPANIES BRAGGING ABOUT THEIR EMPLOYEES

"she has extensive experience in" keyword
"he has extensive experience in" keyword phrase
("he is" OR "she is") "subject matter expert" keyword
" * has been researching * for * years"

EXPERTS SHARING THEIR EXPERTISE

"about the author" keyword
"about the writer" keyword phrase
"is the author of * " keyword
" * has written several " keyword

NOTE: This is one of my favorite search strategies! Just sayin'…
One thing I have noticed about using wildcards in a natural language search
is that you can have up to 3 wildcards in a search. Any more than that and
you get nothing back in return. And it typically works best when your search
is in quotes. For example…

"I developed * software for * and * mobile devices"

…

DUH!

I almost forgot to share something with you concerning search. Glad I
remembered. Of course, you wouldn't have known if I didn't just tell you.
Double duh!

…

In the search string below, I am looking for an old resume of a PhD
student well-versed in oncology. Why an old one? Well, for one, less
competition as most recruiters are only looking for new ones. For two, since
fewer recruiters are looking for them, maybe the candidate won't feel so
hassled when I call. For three, I am taking an educated guess that this might
be a perfect candidate for my needs now if they were at a certain point in
their career back then. (wink) But, I digress…

After doing the search below, I want more options to explore. Just
beneath the search box is a link called "Search Tools" that you might not
have paid much attention to in the past. (See the arrow pointing to it?)

Clicking that link causes three additional links to appear: **a**) Any Time, **b**) All Results and **c**) Search near. By clicking the "Any Time" link, I can refine my search results to those web pages that Google has found in the past hour, past 24 hours, past week, etc. (see opposite page) If I wanted to find results that Google added to its database in the past 24 hours, I would choose the "Past 24 Hours" link.   By the way, I often refine my searches to past week or so when looking for fresh resumes. Just fyi...

Check out the "All results" link. Clicking that link will bring more opportunities to refine your search. Among the choices is "Sites with Images" which can be very handy when sourcing diversity candidates. (Just a suggestion...) Let's take a closer look at this option.

I would not use the "Sites with Images" refinement to find resumes. I would however use it to find people featured on company websites. (Smile) In this example, I am looking for a CTO who works in the auto industry. Once I have a name, the company page will (no doubt) give me a phone number I can. How easy is that?

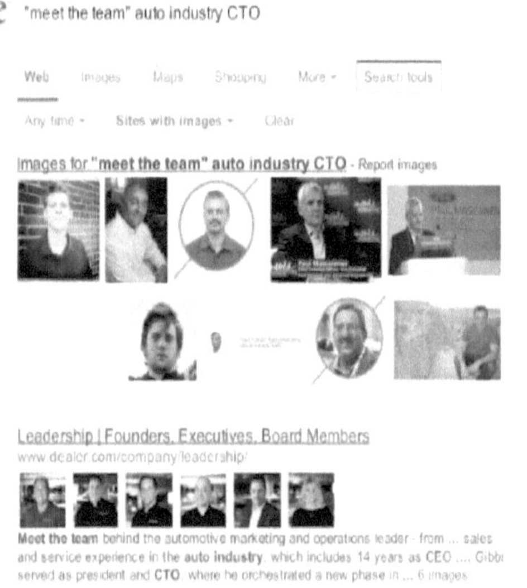

Returning to my previous search for a PhD student for a moment, by choosing the refinement of "Related searches," Google suggests more keywords and phrases I can search on based on what I am presently searching. (As indicative by the arrow below.)

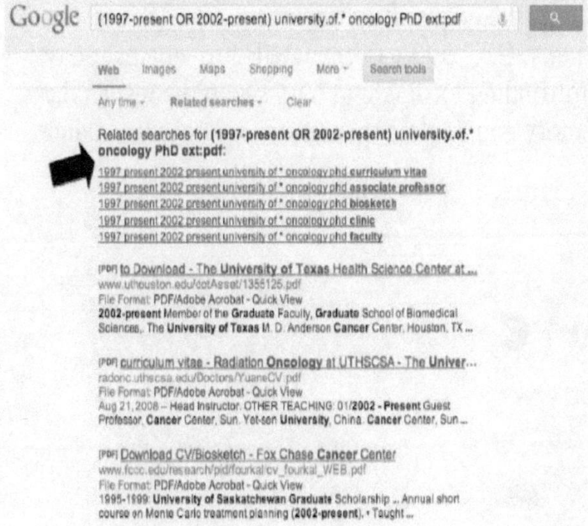

By refining the search by "Reading level" I am able to sift the results by, well… reading level. It makes sense that most of these results are on an advanced reading level since I am looking for a PhD. I don't use this refinement much but when I do, my assumption is that this search returns more learned candidates. Or rather, the ones that use fancier terms.   ;-)

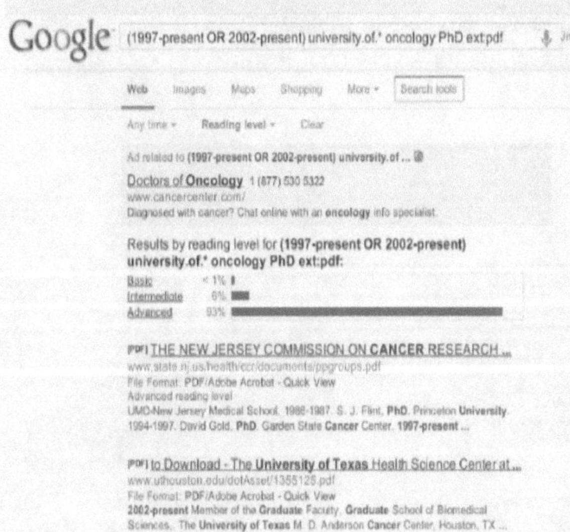

Choosing the "Nearby" link (**a**) switches things up a bit. An additional option appears where you can refine your results by City (**b**), State or Region. My IP address tipped Google off to my location as Atlanta, Ga. However, by clicking "Atlanta, GA" (**c**) I can change that to whatever city I want. This is a great tool for finding local talent! You see in the results the resumes found are from Emory and Spelman which are colleges in Atlanta.

Refining my results to "Translated foreign pages" comes in handy when looking for candidates in other countries. By clicking the "Add language" link (see arrow above) I am able to translate to even more languages. Thank you Google for a very cool feature!

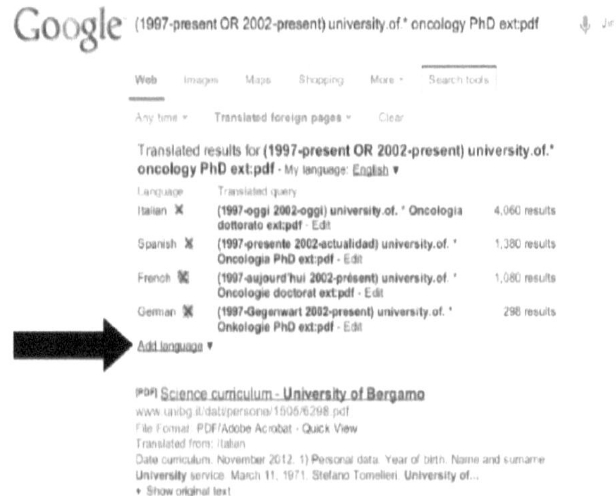

The "Verbatim" searches for exactly what you are looking for and does not include synonyms or related terms based on what it thinks you are looking for. In this example, I am looking for a student who has misspelled the word "oncology" on their resume. Definitely a small number of candidates but nevertheless, candidates that have been overlooked by my competitors as well.

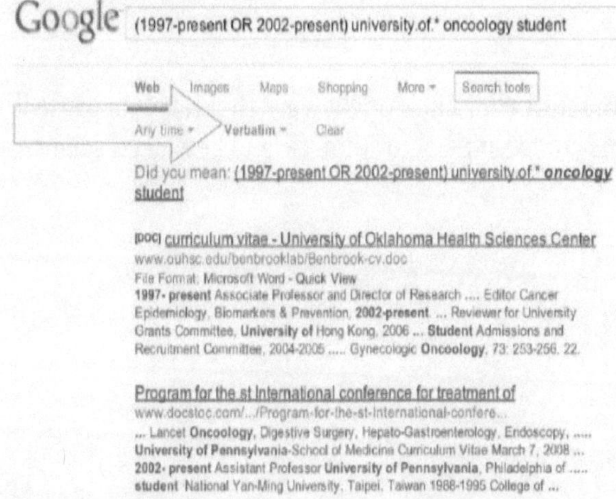

NOT TO SELF: Hmm... I wonder if they know about the other resources on Google that can be leveraged for sourcing purposes?

GOOGLE BOOKS

I want to take you through a demo of how I would use Google Books to find passive candidates. In this example, I am looking for someone with a background in pediatric sonography. The strategy is simple enough. Basically, I look for books on the subject and then focus on who the author is. If they can write a book on the subject, I can assume that they are an expert and quite possibly, someone I want to recruit. Make sense?

To get to Google Books, I go to the address above: http://books.google.com

When the results are returned, I click on the very first result because it came up in my eenie-meenie-minee-moe algorithm. (Pretty advanced science, huh?)

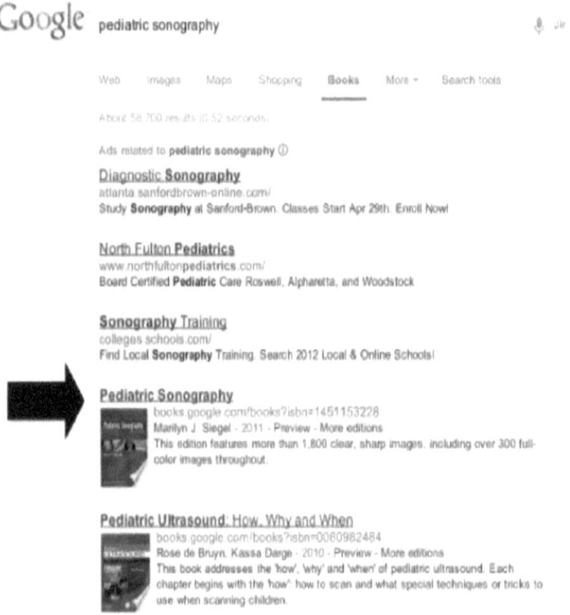

Google will take you to an excerpt of that book that features your keyword. Click the "About this Book" link on the left. (As indicated by the arrow.)

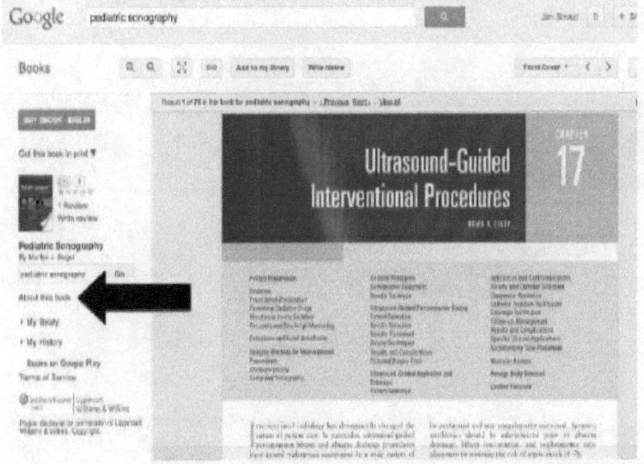

Scroll down the page until you see the "Contributors" section. Click that link.
(As shown by the arrow below.)

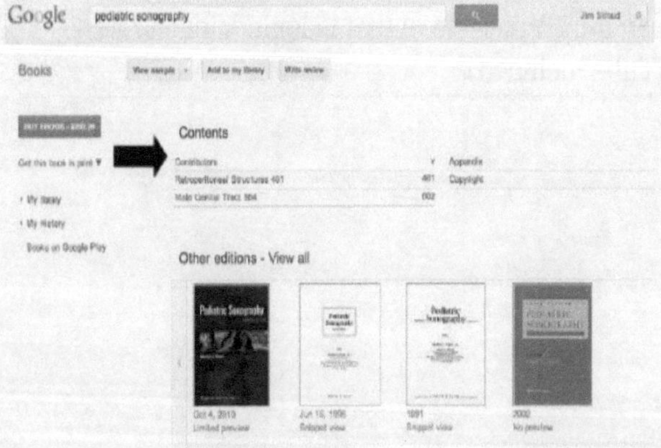

Voila! Five people who know enough about pediatric sonography to write a book. All books do not have a contributor section but most likely have an "About the Author" section where there is some biographical information. In many cases, these sections cite where they are currently working. (wink) Good luck!

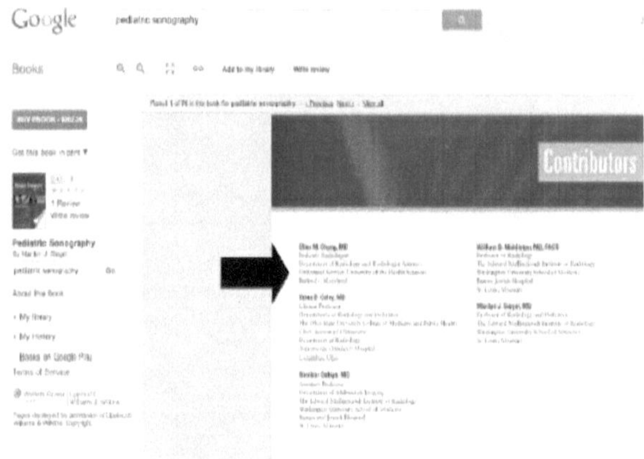

GOOGLE VIDEOS

    I want to take you through a demo of how I would use Google Videos to find passive candidates. And just as a side note, searching Google Video has its advantages over searching YouTube in that Google Video searches multiple video sites (YouTube included).

    I search Google Video using natural language search. I just try to imagine phrases someone might say that would interest me from a sourcing point of view. For example, I can hear someone introducing someone on camera. Say… John Doe, he is a software engineer and he will be reviewing this product. (Or something more or less like that, which is the reasoning behind the search below.)

In the screenshot below, I am doing for a CTO. The great thing about searching Google Videos is that I can find where executives are being interviewed about their company or a topic related to their company.

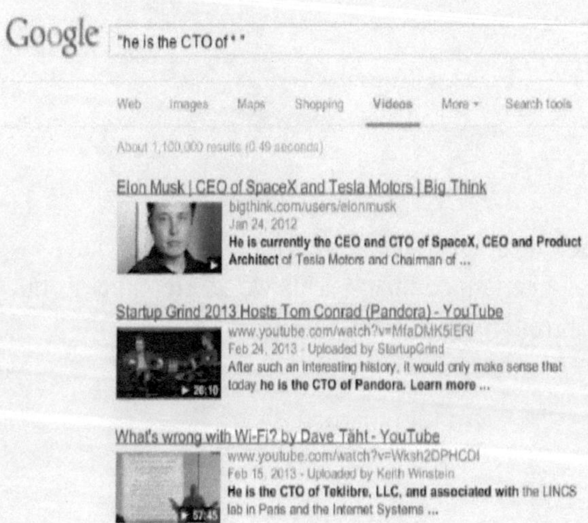

Below are a few more searches you might want to experiment with. Where you see the word "keyword" or "keyword phrase," simply change to something relevant to your recruiting needs.

" * is the CTO of * " keyword

" he is the CFO of * " keyword phrase

" she has extensive experience in * " keyword

" (he OR she) has created * for the * industry" keyword

"as a "job title" (he OR she) * "

 " * was recently promoted to * " keyword

" (he OR she OR they) developed a process * " keyword

" * was instrumental in * " keyword

As I think about it, these searches would also work well on Google Blog Search.

google.com/blogsearch

See what I mean? Below is a search on blogs for people who have been introduced as a CTO of a certain company. This works great, but its not the only way I would source from blogs.

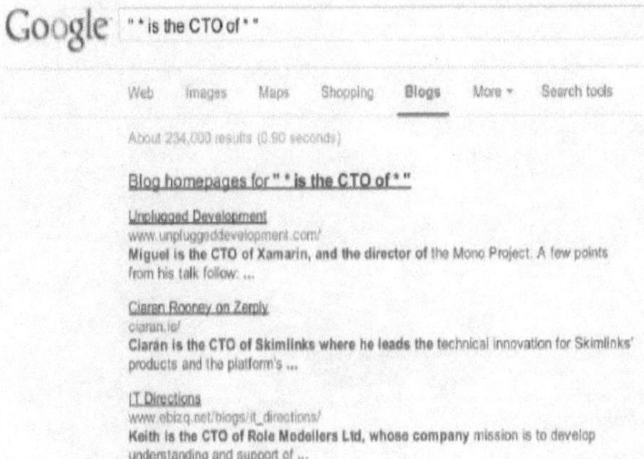

Bloggers (more often than not) have an "About Me" section where they will cite their professional background. In the search below, I am looking for "About Me" info and adding the word "programmer" to find bloggers who describe themselves as Programmers. If not that, at least they have that word on their self-description.

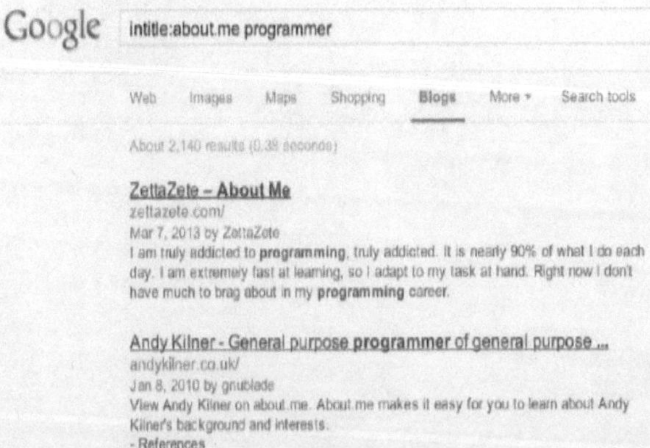

FYI, other searches you might want to try on Google Blog Search are:

intitle:my.profile keyword

intitle:profile ("contact me" OR "email me" OR "call me at")
 keyword

Natural language searching is also great when it comes to searching "Discussions." When you refine your search results by "Discussions," you are asking Google to concentrate the search to online forums.

And while I am looking at further ways to refine searches, one option I want to steer you towards is the "Patents" search. In the example above, I am looking up the term "News Feed Optimization." I choose "Patents" from under the "More" link.

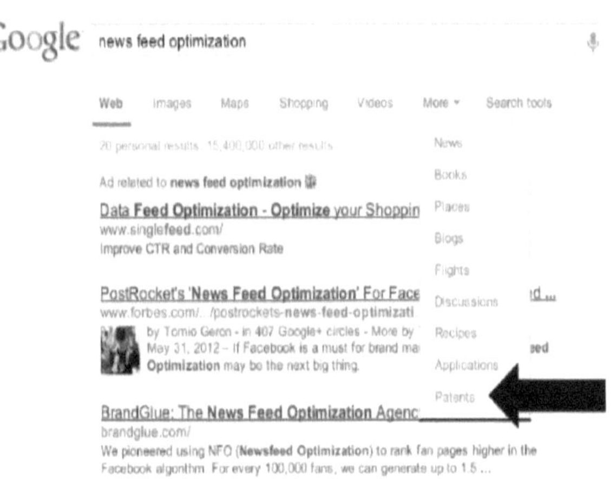

In the search results you can see the names of those who applied for the patent. If they are skilled enough in something to file a patent for it, maybe you might want to hire them? (Smile) In a lot of cases you can see where they worked because the patent is filed on behalf of a company. If the name of the company is not revealed, further research will be necessary. (Maybe they are on LinkedIn?)

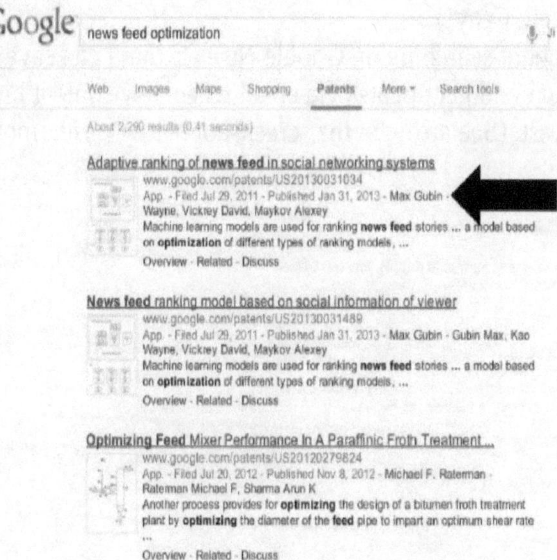

In the example below, I am looking for the mention of someone working as a software engineer at some company. I refine my search by "News," as shown above, by clicking the "News" link (indicated by the arrow).

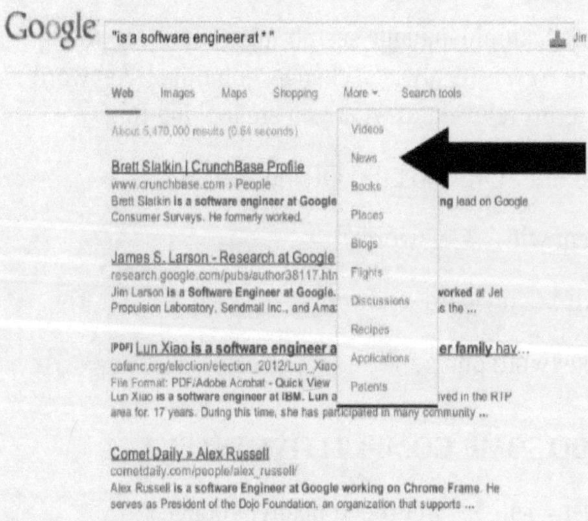

And in the search results, I see 3 recent articles citing software engineers in the news. More often that not, the company they work for will be cited in the article as well. (Yay!)

The added bonus about searching on Google News is that I can save my search as a Google Alert and get updates via email when new content hits the news that fits my interest. (See arrow in the screenshot below.) But, more on Google Alerts later.

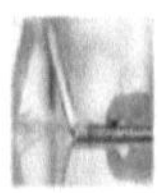

Here are a few more natural language search suggestions for you to experiment with on Google News. As always, change "job title," "keyword" and "keyword phrase" to terms relevant to what you are looking for.

"new role as" ("job title" OR "job title" OR "job title")

"said her department will * " keyword

"said his group will * " keyword

"according to * " keyword phrase

CARE TO DO SOME COMPETITIVE INTEL?

" * said that company will * "   intitle:company.product

WHO IS LAYING OFF PEOPLE YOU WANT TO RECRUIT?

"* said that * will * "   intitle:layoffs   keyword

WHO IS DISCUSSING SALES TRENDS IN NEW YORK?

intitle:sales ("he said" OR "She said" OR "according to")
trends   source:nytimes

WHAT IS THE NEXT BIG THING? WANT TO RECRUIT AN INNOVATOR?

"patent pending technology"

…

NOTE TO SELF: Okay at this point, I am wondering if I should continue with more data. On one hand, I've already given you a lot to digest and practice with. And on the other, I feel the search geek in me begging to unleash more data. Hmm… Shall I stop or "geek" out more? I think at this point I will say… GEEKS RULE!

…

At one point or another, it happens to all Sourcers and Recruiters. You've done all the boolean searching you know how to do and now, you feel stuck. This happens to me quite a bit and I welcome it because it encourages me to experiment. It is not difficult for me to get so consumed into a search and trying new things that I forget what I was looking for initially. (Yes, I really am a geek that way.) Case in point, let me share with you a thought process I had the other day.

I was training some recruiters and picked up on something I think most recruiters overlook. When looking for resumes, they tend to search exclusively for PDF documents or Microsoft Word documents. However, there are several filetype formats that are findable on the web. (Is "findable" a word?) And for that matter, are PDFs and DOCs the most popular file formats for resumes? I mean, I assume that because that's all I tend to see. But, is that really the case?

Time to geek! Excuse me as I mull things over in my mind.

Hmm… No matter what I search on, Google will give you at most 1,000 results. I should make some search strings that will show as many resumes as possible and that do not target any particular industry. I will then narrow those findings down by targeting resumes of various filetypes. Yeah, that makes sense. Right?

Hmm…

(intitle:resume.of OR intitle:resume.by OR intitle:resume.for OR intitle:my.resume OR intitle:"*'s resume") inurl:resume (present OR current) (education OR university.of) -template -submit -apply -openings

In the above search, I am looking for a resume that will have (most likely) "resume of John Doe" OR "resume by John Doe" OR someone who has titled their resume "my resume" OR "John Doe's Resume") The results will have the term "resume" in the URL and words common on a resume like "present" or "current" and… I think you get it from here. (Smile)

The end result was not a flood of resumes as I had hoped. There were a lot of articles about writing resumes and other such career related advice. However, I was pleased with what happened when I refined my search to focus on specific filetypes. For example, in the following search string, my focus is on resumes that are in PDF format. I do this by looking for documents that have "resume.pdf" in the URL.

(intitle:resume.of OR intitle:resume.by OR intitle:resume.for OR intitle:my.resume OR intitle:"*'s resume") **inurl:resume.pdf** (present OR current) (education OR university.of) -template -submit -apply -openings

Based on the results from this and other search strings focused on other formats, the most popular resume formats are:

1) HTML
2) HTM
3) PHP
4) PDF
5) DOC
6) DOCX
7) SHTML
8) ASP
9) RTF

10) CGI

Hmm… That's interesting. I wonder which domains have the most resumes on them? If I wanted to gauge that, how would I? I suppose I would run a search (similar to the one I just did) and refine my searches by top-level domain. Yeah, that makes sense. And since the most popular format for resumes is HTML, I will make that a focus as well. Let me show you what I mean, just to be sure I have not lost you.

```
(intitle:resume.of OR intitle:resume.by OR intitle:resume.for
OR intitle:my.resume OR intitle:"*'s resume")
inurl:resume.html (present OR current) (education OR
university.of)  -template -submit -apply -openings
site:info
```

The above search string is looking for resumes as I have before. The only difference is, by adding "site:info" I am looking at results that are hosted on a ".info" domain. For example, notice the URL in the search result below?

Resume of Tomoko Adachi
astromoko.info/Resume.html
Education & Current Position: Engineer, Code 553. Detector System ...
Greenbelt, MD. Physics Department, Catholic University of America

Based on the results from this and other search strings, these are the top domains ranked by number of resumes hosted. 90% were on the .COM domain. Zowie!

1) .COM
2) .EDU
3) .NET
4) .ORG
5) .WS
6) .INFO
7) .US
8) .BIZ
9) .ME
10) .CC

MOST POPULAR WAY RESUME IS SPELLED ONLINE

\# Resume is the most popular way to spell resume.
\# Resumé is the second most popular way to spell resume.
\# Résumé is the third popular way to spell resume.

(And just in case you are wondering, I use the "Verbatim" refinement to look for exact spellings in the title of documents.)

And while I am on that subject… Wait! Did I answer the question I was trying to figure out initially? Let me flip back a couple of pages and see. (Smile)

Ah! This all started around me suggesting things you can do when you get stuck on a search. Maybe I should just list a bunch of search strings for my readers to play with? I wonder if they would like that? Hm… Decisions, decisions, decisions… Let me think a sec'.

…

NOTE TO SELF: Hmmm… We're getting pretty close to the end of the book. I will… I know… Share a few cool tools that will help them manage all of the data they will find online. Yeah, good idea. Go with that.

…

Not sure you are aware of this, but Google keeps a copy of your search history. If you are concerned about privacy, no one has access to your search history but you. To get to your Google Web History, go to:
https://accounts.google.com/Login?service=hist

Google

Web History

With Web History, you'll be able to:

View and manage your web activity.
You know that great web site you saw online and now can't find? From now on, you can. With Web History, you can view and search across the full text of the pages you've visited, including Google searches, web pages, images, videos and news stories. You can also manage your web activity and remove items from your web history at any time.

Get the search results most relevant to you.
Web History helps deliver more personalized search results based on the things you've searched for on Google and the sites you've

Sign in

Email
████████@gmail.com

Password

Sign in

Web History 1

Once you are logged in, click the "Account Activity" link in the left sidebar. Once you are on Account Activity, scroll down the page until you reach the "Web History" section. Click that section. Once on the "Web History" page, you will see stats about your search activity on Google.

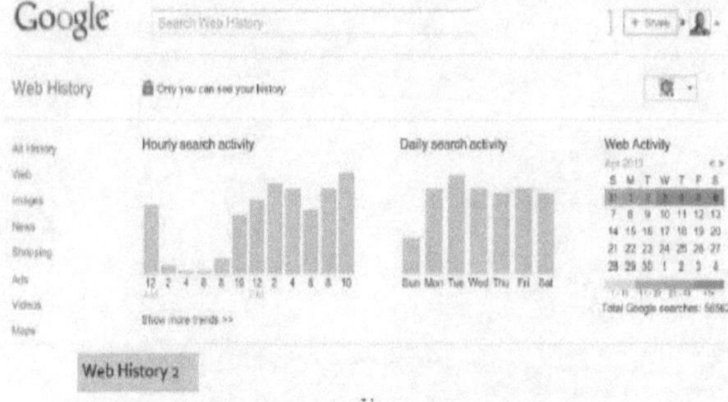

Web History 2

Scrolling down the page will reveal your most recent searches. (An example is shown below).

Mar 12, 2013

Searched for intitle:Resumé		11:55pm
Searched for Resume		11:54pm
Searched for (intitle:resume.of OR intitle:resume.by OR intitle:resume.for OR intitle:my.resume OR intitle:"'s resume") inurl:resume.html (present OR current) (education OR university.of) -template -submit -apply -openings		11:20pm
Searched for (intitle:resume.of OR intitle:resume.by OR intitle:resume.for OR intitle:my.resume OR intitle:"'s resume") inurl:resume.php (present OR current) (education OR university.of) -template -submit -apply -openings		10:48pm
Searched for (intitle:resume.of OR intitle:resume.by OR intitle:resume.for OR intitle:my.resume OR intitle:"'s resume") inurl:resume.pdf (present OR current) (education OR university.of) -template -submit -apply -openings		10:46pm
Searched for (intitle:resume.of OR intitle:resume.by OR intitle:resume.for OR intitle:my.resume OR intitle:"'s resume") inurl:resume (present OR current) (education OR university.of) -template -submit -apply -openings		10:46pm
Searched for (intitle:resume.of OR intitle:resume.by OR intitle:resume.for OR intitle:my.resume OR intitle:"'s resume") inurl:resume (present OR current) (education OR university.of) -template -submit -apply		10:44pm
Searched for (intitle:resume.of OR intitle:resume.by OR intitle:resume.for OR intitle:"'s resume") inurl:resume (present OR current) (education OR university.of) -template -submit -apply		10:42pm
Searched for intitle:resume.of	intitle:resume.by	intitle:resume.for	intitle:"'s resume" inurl:resume.wps (present | current) (education | university.of) -template -submit -apply		10:33pm

At the top of the Web History page is a search box. Simply add keywords and phrases and you will find information of search queries you have done in the past that included those keywords and phrases. You will also see the dates of those searches and the links you clicked on.

How I would use this cool tool:

\# Keeping track of old search strings.
\# Looking up web pages I clicked on in the past.
\# Monitoring how much time I spend on Google.
\# If I add to my calendar that I worked on a certain job on a certain

day, I can look up the searches I performed on that day and gauge how productive I was with my Google searches. Did I click on a lot of links? Did I do a lot of searches on Google?

Of course, this works well if you search alone. However, I bet most of you reading this, work in groups with other sourcers and recruiters. Am I right? I think I am, which is why I am recommending one of my all-time favorite tools - Diigo. Diigo is a toolbar that lets you bookmark and annotate what you find on the web. (Love 'em! Mean it.) Download the Diigo toolbar now! (www.diigo.com)

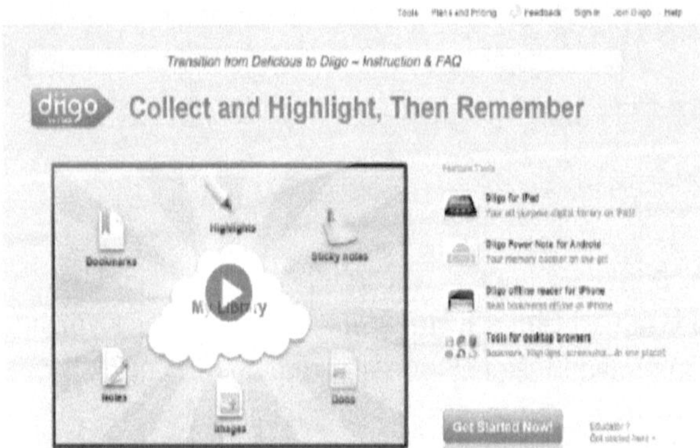

Why do I like it so much? Principally for these three reasons:

1. When I find a resume, a LinkedIn profile or a news article that I like, I can bookmark it for later review. I can also annotate it, leave sticky notes on it and highlight parts of it as if it were a real piece of paper.

2. I can keep all of my bookmarks private, public, or make them accessible to a select group of people. This is EXTREMELY useful because it cuts down on recruiters in my group reaching out to the same people. (How would that work? When someone finds a resume online they will see that someone has already bookmarked the resume and move on to source elsewhere. That is, assuming that they are a member of the group I created. As such, we can see each other's notes on resumes, but no one else can. Not even the author of the resume!)

3. I can create a database, bookmark my search strings and refer to them later. (Yay!)There is much more you can do with Diigo beyond what I shared. I highly suggest that you check out their YouTube channel which has a lot of tutorials on it. http://www.youtube.com/diigobuzz

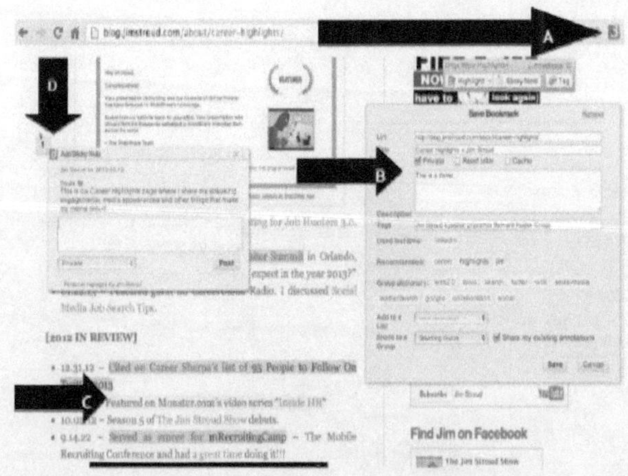

I wanted to give you a glimpse into what its like to work with Diigo.

The red ribbon over the Diigo icon (**a**) lets me know that a bookmark has been made on this page. I see that ribbon because I made the bookmark or, someone in a group I am a member of has made this bookmark or, the bookmark is public and visible to all.

By clicking the Diigo icon, I can see the notes that were made in the bookmark (**b**) and how it was tagged.

Using Diigo's highlighter pen (**c**), I can mark up the parts of the page that I think are most significant.

By mousing over the sticky note icon (**d**), I can see the notation left

behind by myself or others.

GOOGLE ALERTS

I mentioned Google Alerts earlier when I was discussing how to search the news using natural language. I love me some Google Alerts! Why? It lets me put my sourcing on automatic. Back in the day, I would run some web search strings and go through the results later. Unfortunately, Google won't let me save web searches anymore. (Sad face) However, I can do a search on everything else: Blogs, News, Video, Discussions and Books.

I suggest setting up your alert notifications for once a week. Otherwise, you may get too many Google Alerts in email to manage efficiently. Umm.. Depending on how many you have set up. I think I used to have 100 or so set up when I could use it to search the web. But hey, that's just me. (Insert smile here)

WOW!

According to InternetWorldStats.com there are a bazillion people on the internet! Okay, 7+ Billion people to be more exact. Quite a few of them can be found online using the methods I am sharing in this book. However, a larger segment can be found via creative Employment Branding, Social Networks, New Media and a host of other methods.

Contact me and the good folks over at Bernard Hodes Group! We have a lot of training options available to share with you. Among them: Recruiting with LinkedIn, Recruiting with Facebook, Recruiting with Google Plus and Recruiting with Twitter. Just FYI…

Bernard Hodes Group: www.hodes.com/ 888-438-9911 / info@hodes.com

…

GUESS WHAT?

You made it to the end of this book. Thanks for sticking it out. As a way of saying thank you for getting this far, I am going to share with you a few more search strings and situations for when I would most likely use them. I hope they prove useful.

…

I'm not having much luck finding a resume of someone who is an authority in (whatever). So, as a recourse, I look for (whatever) and add emails to my search. Maybe I will get lucky and find someone who is willing to be contacted regarding (whatever) and I can recruit them.

```
(email.me OR contact.me)    ("*@gmail.com" OR
"*@hotmail.com" OR "*@yahoo.com"    OR
"*@outlook.com")  keyword –intitle:jobs
```

Hmm… Maybe I should go with actual examples instead of just saying "whatever." Let's see how that works. Okay. Let's say that you are looking for a "Facilities Manager" for an opportunity in the manufacturing industry. And for fun, let's say that this req is an old one and most likely, your org has found all the resumes they are going to find online. (Or, at least they feel that way.) One thing is certain, there are companies out there who hire Facilities Managers. What do they all have in common? Well, one thing for sure, they all have websites. And on said websites, it's a good bet that they have an "About Us" page. Such being the case, I look for company "About Us" pages that have the term "Facilities Manager" posted therein.

Booyah! Here are a couple of examples of what I find: Mauricio Cardoso and Ray Porter.

Tarrant Area Food Bank - **About Us** - Staff
www.tafb.org/staff.html
Risk Management & **Facilities Manager** - Mauricio Cardoso. Allocation Specialist –
Linda ... **Warehouse** Manager - Benny Garcia. Logistics & Receiving ...

Staff | **About Us** | CARITAS
www.caritasva.org/aboutus_new_staff.html
Ray Porter, **Facilities Manager** (804) 230-1217. James Taylor, Facilities/ ... Michael
Gordon, Warehouse Procurement Manager (804) 343-5008. Julie Johnson ...

And here are some search strings I would use to find more of the same.

intitle:about.us (manufacturing | warehouse) "facilities manager"

intitle:about manufacturing "facilities manager" (he | she)
-intitle:job

"Facilities Manager" intitle:staff manufacturing -intitle:jobs
-submit -apply

"* is the Facilities Manager at * " warehouse

"Facilities Manager" intitle:our.people manufacturing
-intitle:jobs -submit -apply

intitle:team "facilities manager * " manufacturing

Now, I will look for some college students with an academic focus on computer science. I will also insure that the results I find are geared towards students graduating in 2013.

" (projected OR expected OR prospective OR estimated)
graduation.date * 2013 " education (email OR phone) (intitle:vitae
OR intitle:resume) computer.science

I am imagining now that I am looking for some executives who work for a company in the consumer electronics industry. Principally I want a "Vice President of Marketing" but, I am open to other senior management types as well. Here are some search strings I would use to find them. Since they are natural language searches, I try them on Google News as well.

" * joins * as Senior VP" "consumer electronics"

" * promoted to *" "consumer electronics"

" * hires * as Director of" "consumer electronics"

" * named * VP of * "   "consumer electronics"

" * approves promotion of * "   electronics

" * welcomes * as VP "   "consumer electronics"

" * announces * VP of * " "consumer electronics"

" * appoints * VP of * "   "consumer electronics"

As I think about it, I could look for Executives another way as well. How? I could look for articles and blog posts they've written. To do that, I run the following search strings.

about.the.writer " * is the (CEO OR founder OR VP)"
"consumer electronics"

intitle:about.the.author " * is vice president of "
"consumer electronics"

"about the author"   " * is vice president of "   "consumer
electronics"

Let me switch gears a bit and give you something else to consider when sourcing. Every industry has a newsletter, magazine or some sort of publication associated with it. If you can find such a resource relevant to the industry you are looking for, you might find some leads. After all, featured in the articles of those publications are quotes from people in the field and/or an interview of some kind. Get me? Here are a few search strings for tracking down engineers who work in… umm… Sanitation.

```
intitle:sanitation (intitle:magazine | intitle:quarterly |
intitle:journal | intitle:news | intitle:newsletter) " * an
engineer "
```

```
intitle:report  water.and.sanitation   " (he OR she) is an
engineer"
```

```
inurl:news  ~sanitation   " (he OR she) is an engineer"
```

Now, let's go on to something different. Earlier in the book, I gave a list of suggestions on how to compile a list of competitor (and related) companies to target with your searches. I want to suggest one more strategy. Consider recruiting out of companies being heralded as producers of award-winning products. Who knows? You might discover an innovative startup with talent ripe for the picking. Here are a few search strings for finding innovative companies in Cloud Computing.

```
intitle:award.winning   niche   "cloud computing"
```

```
intitle:best.of  "cloud computing"   (award OR  honored OR
won)
```

```
(intitle:award.winning OR intitle:nominated.for  OR
intitle:best.of.breed) "cloud computing"
```

If you like this strategy, a few more words you might want to play with in your searches are: "Top 100," "Best Companies" and "Fastest Growing."

…

Umm… I am beginning to feel like I am rambling, so let me close out with two more tactics that can prove useful to you.

…

There are several websites available that allow users to store documents online for free. For example, Google has "Google Drive" (formerly "Google Docs") which lets people upload all kinds of content to a virtual drive. Most of the things people upload is for their private use. However, there are quite a few pieces of content out there made available to the public. Among them, resumes. Check out what I see when I site search Google Docs.

Below are search strings for finding Software Engineer resumes on sites where users can upload documents and make them available to the public (for free, by the way.)

site:scribd.com intitle:resume present education "software engineer"

site:docstoc.com intitle:resume (education | university.of) software.engineer -sample -template

site:slideshare.net intitle:resume (education | university.of) software.engineer -sample -template

You might be wondering how I target sites like "docstoc.com" and mine it for resumes. Well, it's a simple formula. So simple that I perform it subconsciously, basically:

I scan search results to see which URLs appear more than once.

I site search to see if Google has indexed a large number of the site's pages.

I visit the site where the leads are coming from.

I look for words or phrases that would most likely appear on all (or most) pages on that website.

I create searches based on webpage commonalities and begin mining for leads.

Hmm… let me do a real life example to bring this point home even further. Let's say I am still looking for a Software Engineer. Among the results, I see the following:

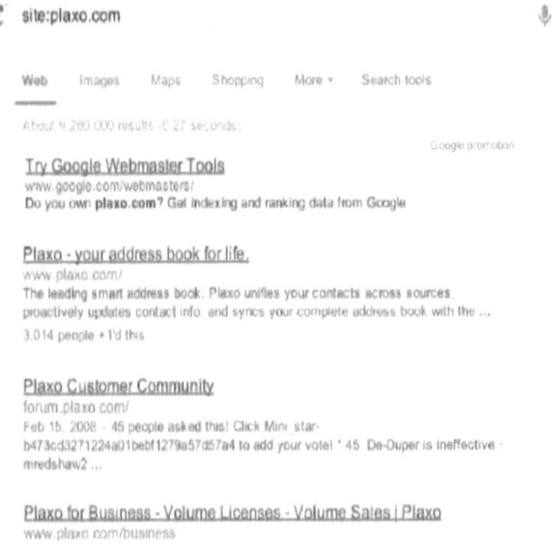

The first thing I notice is the title. It has the words "Public Profile" in it and someone's name. More than likely all of their profile pages are set up that way. I also see the words "profile" and "showPublic" are in the URL. Finally, I see that the result is from plaxo.com. I wonder how many pages Google has in its database from Plaxo.com?

Hmm… Google says that they have 9+ million of Plaxo's webpages indexed. Good to know. Why? Since so much data is stored, I am confident I will find something when I look. But first, let me gather a bit more intel by visiting the profile I found initially.

Oh! Before I continue, let me give you a heads up on something. Should you ever see in your results words like: "pages," "members," "profile," "home," "homepage" or "my," then chances are that website is a good candidate for being mined for leads the way I am demonstrating now with Plaxo. Just FYI…

Okay, I digress.

Once on Mr. Bodhuin's profile, I look for things that might be on other Plaxo profiles. Things like the (**a**) "Me on the Web" module in the sidebar, (**b**) how many connections he has, how sections of the profile are named. For example (**c**) "Professional Summary," (**d**) "Work/Education," (**e**) "Work Experience" and further down the page (not shown above) "Education" and "Public Stream."

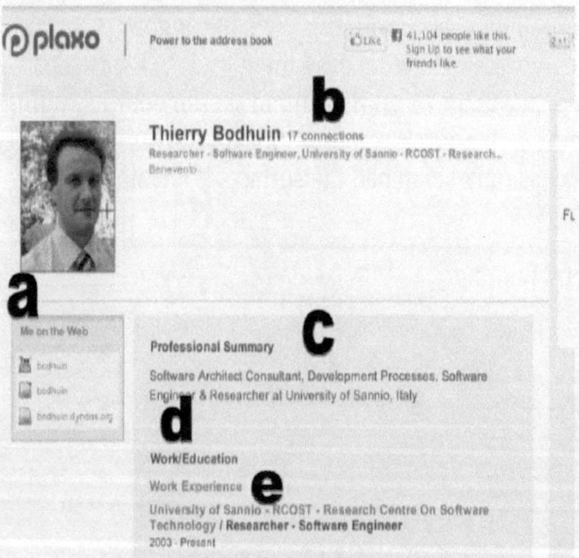

Armed with that data, I begin experimenting with search strings to see which give me the most and/or best results. Just for the sake of your curiosity, here are some of the searches I performed and the results.

site:plaxo.com intitle:public.profile [14.500 results]

site:plaxo.com "software engineer" [42,400 results]

site:plaxo.com inurl:profile "software engineer" [13,500 results]

site:plaxo.com inurl:profile "Work/Education" "software engineer" [8 results]

site:plaxo.com   "Work Experience" "software engineer" [14 results]

site:plaxo.com intitle:public.profile "software engineer" [180 results]

site:plaxo.com "public stream" "software engineer" [8 results]

I noticed that the larger the search results, the more likely I was going to come across pages I did not want to see. Namely, jobs and career advice, etc. This is why its important to experiment! You have to tweak, tweak, tweak to get all the data you can. Make sense? Hope so…

…

Although I have more I can show you, this feels like a good place to stop. Battling my inner search geek is not an easy thing. (wink) Please do keep Bernard Hodes Group (www.hodes.com) in mind should your recruiting organization ever need training in Sourcing and/or Social Recruiting. I promise you that this book has only scratched the surface. (Operators are standing by.)

So, until then, happy hunting!